Babies of the Bible

written by Carolyn Kuykendall
illustrated by Kathryn Hutton

Library of Congress Catalog Card No. 85-62956
© 1986. The STANDARD PUBLISHING Company, Cincinnati, Ohio
Division of STANDEX INTERNATIONAL Corporation. Printed in U.S.A.

Eve was the world's first mother.
She had baby Cain; then Abel his brother.

When Noah was a baby boy,
 he may have had a boat for a toy.

Isaac made his parents glad.
Sarah and Abraham loved the little lad.

A girl named Rebekah was kind and fair. While she was still young, she learned to share.

Jacob and Esau were double the fun.
Their parents liked having more than one.

Esau liked to play outside,
  while Jacob liked to run and hide.

Leah combed baby Rachel's hair.
Babies need a lot of care.

While his baby brother slept nearby, young Joseph was quiet so Benjamin wouldn't cry.

Moses went for a ride in a boat.
Miriam watched to make sure it would float.

Moses was found by Pharaoh's daughter. She brought the baby out of the water.

Obed brought happiness after his birth. Boaz and Ruth were the happiest parents on earth.

Grandmother Naomi felt great joy.
The Lord had sent them a baby boy!

Hannah prayed for a baby son,
 so God decided to send her one.

Samuel loved God when he was a young lad.
This made his mother very glad.

Young David loved God as he grew strong.
He liked to play his harp and sing a song.

Esther was the prettiest baby her family had ever seen.
She grew up to become a beautiful queen.

Elizabeth was pleased to have a son. Zechariah called the baby John.

Mary made Jesus a bed out of straw.
He came to bring peace to one and all.

A man named Simeon was truly blessed. He knew Jesus was different from all the rest.

Some men said to Jesus in the temple one day,
"We're surprised at what you have to say."

Timothy's mother told him Bible stories every day.
She wanted to be sure he grew up the right way.

When you were a baby, still brand-new,
your parents thanked God for sending you.

Thank You, God, for all I see.
Thank You, too, for loving me!